VETERANS MILITARY CIVILIANS

A POSITIVE-LISTENING COURSE BOOK

The Ten-Step Teller and Listener Journey
A Guide for Veterans, Military, and Civilians

"Patriotism comes in many forms.
Listening is one of the great ones."

Developed by Christopher Uzzi , Vietnam Veteran, CRPS:

VETERANS MILITARY CIVILIANS

A POSITIVE-LISTENING COURSE BOOK

The Ten-Step Teller and Listener Journey
A Guide for Veterans, Military, and Civilians

Published in the United States of America by
Veterans Listening Post LLC
Naples, Florida USA
http://www.vlpost.com

ISBN: 0692854649
ISBN 978-0692854648 (Paperback)
ISBN 978-1-5323-3835-9 (E-Book)
Library of Congress Control Number: 2017905293
LCCN Imprint VLP

VMLP/VLP Logo™

~~~~~~~~~~~~~~~

VLP Course Contents

The Mission 1

Dedication 3

Foreword 5

Steady-State Story Power 7

Excellent Listeners 9

Listening-Post Adventure 10

The Ten-Step Course 12

You Can Tell the Future by Listening 14

SECTION ONE 16

Session 1: Sharing 17

I Like Your Hat 20

Session 2: Purpose 22

Listening Directions 24

Session 3: Release 26

Personal and Universal Listening 28

Session 4: Direct 30

The Bus Ride 33

Session 5: Healing 35

SECTION TWO 38

The Neuroscience of Happiness 39

Elements of Well-Being 40

Steady-State Story Process 42

Session of Insight 43

Insight Session 45

SECTION THREE: 47

Basic Training 48

Non-Commissioned Officers Training 50

Session 6: Health 53

Sergeant Rock 56

Session 7: Stability 58

The Saint Christopher Effect 60

SECTION FOUR 62

Session 8: Support 63

Rock Star versus Military 65

Session 9: Confidence 68

Listening to Iraq and Afghanistan Veterans 71

Session 10: Completion 73

Taking Hold of Your Command 76

Bibliography 77

The Listening Post National Guide 78

VLP Programs of Influence 78

On-the-Ground Action 80

VLP Course Continuation 81

Certificate of Support 83

Coach Chris Uzzi 84

VLP Certifications and Services 86

Invitation 88

SUPPORT

The Mission:

CONNECT AND RECOGNIZE

The Military Listening Post

Military forces have historically used listening posts for early warning detection and protection against their opposition for as long as conflicts have existed. When nighttime comes, in a hostile military environment, a unit commander will deploy a manned team some distance beyond the company's fortified perimeter. Their distinct purpose is to protect the main detachment from surprise attacks. The team would have special instructions to listen for sounds and watch for movements that may pose a threat of imminent harm to their military unit. When hostility is detected, the manned team returns to their base to alert the company. The team then uses a password to return to the safety of the unit's fortified area.

The Veterans Listening Post (VLP)

VLP's listening-post mission is to send out passionate and trained civilians, veterans and active military, who want to help in some meaningful way. Their assignment is to connect, and to recognize the power of telling and listening to the stories of veterans and active military. For this vital mission, the password is "COMPASSION!"

Dedication

VLP humbly recognizes the courageous sacrifice of those veterans who paid the ultimate price, giving their lives for the United States of America and the free world. VLP recognizes the loving family, friends and others who have embraced listening to our veterans as they tell their stories. We at VLP recognize the immutable feelings that accompany this journey. The selfless men and women who served their country with honor are the ultimate warriors. They and their stories deserve the highest respect from us all for their service and sacrifice.

VLP recognizes the wounded warriors, those veterans who have experienced traumatic injury, suffering both visible and invisible wounds. These warriors are living examples of supreme courage and bravery. Their heroism has even continued off the battlefield, and is evident through the adversity they continue to overcome in their daily lives. They are the perennial warriors, continuously displaying bravery and perseverance. We at VLP fully support and recognize these warriors. We owe you an enduring debt of gratitude. We are eternally grateful for your service and your sacrifices.

This book is entitled: Veterans-Military-Civilians. VLP will demonstrate to all veterans and active military that we ARE listening to YOU. We at VLP recognize, with great honor, the many support services that are steadfastly performed in the military, services such as; humanitarian projects, engineering, construction, intelligence, safety, administration services, supply services and Foreign Service. They also include mental health services, family support services, sports teams, drill teams, hospital staff and medical specialists. We also want to recognize drone specialists, IT specialists, marching bands, military police, JAG, Special Forces, Air Force, Army, Navy, Marines, National Guard, Coast Guard, ship crews, pilots, infantry, cooks, and all the other effective and vital services that are required to provide us with the freedom we all hold so very dear.

To you, our military who are presently serving, VLP conveys our deepest respect and gratitude for the strength and dedication you continue to display while protecting United States citizens as well as the remainder of the free world.

Thank you to all the storytellers for the heartfelt personal stories that you have shared with us in this book. You have provided the inspiration for the transformative effect that this book will have for every future reader. Thank you also to all the listeners for the depth of compassion you've shown to our Veterans, our active military and to us here at VLP. We appreciate your supportive feedback. When you, as a listener, take your valuable time to listen to another's story, you demonstrate your patriotism and offer others important opportunities for solid transformation.

This is a simple, yet valuable experience for not only the storyteller, but also the listener, as they discover the human aspects of a tale which may deeply relate to their own life. The experience imbues both parties with fresh, and oftentimes rejuvenating perspective, bringing with it a newfound clarity derived from the opportunity to feel truly connected to someone else with the ability to relate. You are not alone. Thank you to each and every one of you who are reading this book. We invite you to become a VLP listener.

Foreword

An insight meditation instructor once said, "The person who goes into meditation is not the same person who comes out of meditation." That person receives beneficial changes in health and understanding about themselves and within themselves. When you read this book, as a person who goes through the ten-step course by participating in the listening and storytelling course, you will also be transformed. The reader will gain dynamic insight and a deeper understanding of the value of listening to our veterans and active military.

The word *veteran* means "one who gives service to their country." The word also has a civilian dictionary definition, meaning, a person who has had long service or experience in an occupation or field. Eventually, we all become veterans in our own way.

The US Armed Forces are extremely effective at transforming ordinary people into military experts. This transformation is fundamental for the military's mission to succeed. Just as the military transforms its soldiers, VLP believes that listening to the stories of veterans and active military, with the focus on positive outcomes and opportunities, can transform all who participate in an extraordinarily beneficial way.

Steady-State Story Power

VLP's ten-step course focuses on three power-action words. They are *Turnaround, Uplift* and *Positivity*. These are simple words, yet each one is packed with powerful meaning. *Turnaround* means to view an often traumatic and tough story, in a different way. *Turnaround* denotes the ability to look past the negative and find the encouraging parts of a story as its takeaway. Every story has the potential for a turnaround. Sometimes one must look with firmness and resolve, yet it's always there. *Uplift* means working with proactive effort, to support in a positive way. *Uplift* can best be accomplished by accessing your own inner resources of intention and inspiration as well as employing whatever external resources may be available to you, such as family, friends and organizations which provide uplifting services. *Positivity* is the process of always adding changes that are good for your well-being. These three words are the working avenues to the healing, healthy and happy outcomes of the Ten-Step Steady-State Story course by VLP.

Positive stories generate what VLP calls *steady-state story power.* This dynamic occurs when positive aspects of one's story uplifts and inspires not only the storyteller, but all those who listen to the story as well. When we embrace the positive aspects of a story, we can adopt the context of the story and apply its positive messages and uplifting influences to that of our own life story. Through the ten-step resource guide's sessions, we will learn to create our own positive story. Through the creation of your own encouraging story, we will in turn help those who listen to your story. These listeners are then inspired to look at their own life stories more optimistically, taking positive aspects of the teller's story and applying them to their own life stories.

As you read the following personal and universal listening stories, you will recognize aspects and similarities of your own story. Listening to others will assist and guide you in your personal evolution toward creating a more positive personal life story.

Excellent Listeners

All of us have the capability to become excellent listeners. To pursue our goals in life, we had to subconsciously employ various methods of listening. Those methods provided us with a progressive stream of achievements that we attained through simple listening. The ten-step guided process of telling and listening will produce a standard of stability for veterans, military and all readers as this course unfolds.

The teller and listener sessions are known as *sessions of positive influence*. Sessions of positive influence are the story segments that we want to focus on. The stories that we will listen to in this course book are stories of bravery, endurance, skill and passionate effort in everyday life. As you read these stories, you may say to yourself, "I like this," or perhaps, "I can relate to that," or "I admire the way the teller tells his or her story." Each topic presents keywords of positive-listening techniques. The keywords in each session help to bring *positive balancing*. Positive balancing is the road to strength and stability that the participants will be able to rely upon for their beneficial outcomes.

Listening-Post Adventure

In The Ten-Step Listening Course, VLP looks for stories which reflect a result which can be considered a dual success, wherein both the teller and the listener benefit from the experience. A teller will benefit from having had the opportunity to share his or her experience with someone who can relate to the tale, and the listener may benefit from hearing something which touches a chord in their own experiences. We know that your military experiences and civilian stories will be personal, at times serious and always authentic. Any humor in our stories will serve to make them more healing, healthy and happy. This is your time to express things that have real meaning to you. No matter whether it is about the past, present or the future, this is the time and the place to tell your story.

Just think of your story like one told in a newspaper. It has a beginning, which can be started from any point during your service or in your civilian life. It has a body, where you describe how much your service meant to you, including the good friendships made or the seemingly endless experiences that you struggled through, and how it was that you did manage to get through it. Your story can be about anything with the potential to eventually bring about a healthy and positive takeaway. Bring your story to a conclusion and into the present. Look for the turnaround, the uplift and the positivity in your tale. Your negative–to-positive story will provide beneficial effects for all who read or listen to it. For the men and women currently serving in the military, it will allow them to draw from the immense strength of others who have been there and done that. With the strength so willingly shared, they will be better prepared to perform their own duties of service.

In the military, the term, *forward march* represents the progress of moving ahead in a strong, purposeful direction. Therefore, recruits, we say:

"Forward March!"

The Ten-Step Course

Course Description

This ten-step curriculum provides participants with a reliable building-block method that is put into practice through the telling of and listening to positive, uplifting, turnaround stories.

Presentation

Course participants attend ten sessions, each adjustable to the group's needs. A full session lasts ninety minutes. Each session covers a specific topic and goal. The course includes class work, homework and fieldwork. The course focuses on both veterans and current military. However, it is a universal course that everyone can attend. For remote attendance and follow-up questions, we employ Skype, social networking, e-mail and texts. Each of these work well within the course structure, as needed.

Objective

The paramount and universal goal throughout each session is to develop and maintain the ten-step skill set that is the steady-state story process.

The sessions produce positive actions and reactions through specific positive resourceful dynamics. This leads to the accomplishment of class objectives. Benefits can be achieved when taking one class session. The benefits multiply and are cumulative with each additional session completed.

Course Structure

The four paradigms of service are: story social, story unity, internal story and sustainable story.

Story social: Shared resources.
Story unity: Many options, external resources.
Internal story: Creating the story that you believe best suits you.
Sustainable story: Continuous turnaround, uplift and positivity.

Story Subjects

VLP uses first names with numbers in this course book for all of the example stories. This keeps the value of the story intact. The focus is on the stories. This makes them universal stories, so that all can see their own stories reflected within them, by connecting their own story to aspects within the example stories.

Course Book

VLP uses the word, *week,* in this course as a suggested time frame. However, any time an opportunity arises is the best time. Participants are given strategic and vital assignments to be completed after class. This connects participants with solid resources of assistance. Participants are encouraged to include an outside person or persons as a listening buddy, as part of the course structure.

Pass-It-Forward Teaching

The VLP ten-step course provides concrete answers to help veterans organizations, nonprofits, social programs and individual programs to better provide positive transformational results for our veterans and our active military on a right-here, right-now basis. Long after their military service, veterans continue to struggle to absorb the full meaning of their service to their country. This course is built on solid paradigms that support a steady-state story process of positive transformation.

You Can Tell the Future by Listening

A good poker player needs to be skilled in listening and observing "tells." This tends to increase their odds of winning a poker hand. "Tells," to a poker player are their opponent's facial gestures, body language and words that express certain meanings.

Any slight change in a player's behavior or demeanor can give clues that may increase a poker player's odds of winning a poker hand.

Listening works the same way. Time spent listening to our veterans and active military strengthens their collective present story, one that is cherished and appreciated and also where the Vet is recognized for their tremendous bravery and selfless sacrifice. This sense of worth carries on into the future, helping the veterans on their journey. Supportive listening represents "tells" for the military serviceman or servicewoman, which shows them that their services and sacrifices are appreciated. This generates the sentiment that the people they serve strongly support them. This sentiment gives veterans and active military a solid sense of duty and pride that will benefit us all with a stronger military protecting our freedoms and security well into the future.

Think of the times, at a national event, when the announcer says, "Let us pause for a few moments, to recognize the service and sacrifice of all those who have served our country with honor." In the same way you give great honor to those who have served, by pausing and taking the opportunity to listen to their stories, reflecting on the value of the services and sacrifices our veterans have freely given. Recognizing the invaluable service that the military performs, you are partnering with them and setting up a well-planned mission of winning the cause of freedom for the future, simply by listening.

Section One

Session One

SHARING

VLP Guide

Listen to the story below. Transfer your thoughts and personal experiences into this story.

Sharing: Veteran's Story

Hi, Listening Post, this is Charlie 701. After spending six months on the combat lines near the Iraq border, it felt like never-ending days, each day blending into the next. You live with a semi-heightened feeling of mental readiness that burns through you. When I received news and support from home, it always lifted me up when things seemed to be pushing me down.

My platoon buddies kept me in reality with their support. My platoon sergeant and platoon commander were always on level ground; their strong leadership never wavered from mission to mission.

Fitting back into my civilian life has come with its challenges. What I am now calling my "civilian life's mission," is to continue as I did with my training and with the resources I gained from the military. These, in the long run, will serve me well.

Outside circumstances do not disrupt the mental readiness; I learned this during my military service. I adjust and adapt to the course that best suits me. So, this is my story.

I must say, I am very appreciative that someone would take the time to listen. Thanks for the support.

Listener's Story and Response

Charlie 701, this is Gail 313. I'm happy to be one of your listeners. I have read your story twice. It's so encouraging to me. There are so many positive attributes in your description that honor you. Reading your story has given me a better understanding of how things really are on the combat lines and how important receiving news is from loved ones. Your story takes uncertainty, and turns it into certainty. Thank you for your story and the terrific direction that you are going in. I will always be grateful to you and all veterans for your service.

VLP's Response

Charlie 701, you are on the steady-state story process of sharing resources. Your mental fortitude, resilience and choice to create positive outcomes for yourself are an inspiration to all. Thanks for sharing, very steady, Charlie 701.

Discussion Format

Was telling your story a positive sharing experience for you? What statement below expresses your direction? During the week, pause to listen to a story and follow-up with some words of encouragement for the person who was brave enough to share their story with you. Pause and share a story about your service with a family member or a friend.

VLP Sharing Affirmations

1. It felt transformative to share a story with someone who would listen.
2. Telling this story is important for me.
3. Sharing my story means trusting in the listener.
4. Sharing is a wonderful help for me.
5. I like this and it helps me in my journey.

I Like Your Hat

A personal way of recognizing and listening to veterans and military is through their hats. Veterans love their hats. Most veterans have hats which display their branch of service, such as the Air Force, Navy, Army, Marines, National Guard or Coast Guard. Sometimes the actual term of the veteran's service is also displayed on their hats. This is all very good. Be proud of your service and let everyone else be thankful for the service that you provided.

Here's the catch. Sometimes, for a moment, a veteran may forget they are wearing their veteran's hat. A person comes along and says, "Thank you for your service." Sometimes there is silent moment of reaction and adjustment from the veteran before the veteran responds.

A very easy way of giving recognition, when passing by a person who is displaying their military service hat, is to simply say, "Hi! I like your hat." this works very well. It is a very quick and complete saying that brings focus speedily to the hat and recognizes the person's service at the same time.

The veteran wearing the hat is instantly focused on their hat and will respond with a big smile and a grateful, "Thank you." In just those few moments, the veteran receives a positive moment of recognition that you have provided, creating a positive transformative outcome for all.

Session Two

PURPOSE

VLP Guide

The veteran describes the good parts of their military service. The listener listens to their story.

VLP Teller Guide

You are in Session 2. Call on all the parts of your personality that make you shine. Tell your story.

Purpose: Veteran's Story

Hi, VLP, this is Alan 121. My Air Force military experience was the stepping-stone to reaching many of my life goals. I went through intense schooling in various Air Force training centers.

This training gave me the strength to rough out the tough spots and adjust to the middle ground. I gained the confidence to move when things position themselves in a clearer way. My military training was a disciplined journey. It taught me how trustworthy, reliable and professional the training is that the Air Force provides for the men and women serving.

When I fall from grace, which happens very often, I call up that part of my Air Force training and discipline which has proven to help with my outcomes. I hope I make sense. Just the fact that I can express myself, my purpose, and be heard is good for me. Thanks, Listening Post.

Listener's Story and Response

Alan 121, this is Roberto 250. I joined the Listening Post to see what help I could give as a listener. Well, your story has helped me understand what it means to build a support network that I can draw upon from the many positive life experiences that I have experienced.

After I read your story, I decided to go back to the resources that I have acquired such as my good friends and coworkers who have helped me with my issues. Your story was helpful. Thank you. I was supposed to help you by listening. Ha-ha, you ended up helping me!

Discussion Format

What part of your personal story can you express in a positive turnaround way this week? Explore a direction you would like your story to take. Try one of the one-line resets through the VLP affirmation. It's fun to experience and explore the different positive outcomes.

VLP Purposeful Affirmations

1. I have good options and avenues for a turnaround.
2. Purpose will always bring out my positive.
3. I am building more confidence in myself.
4. Purpose gives me an open road.
5. I'm glad I can tell my story.

Listening Directions

Listening directs the conversation. As a listener, you can say to a veteran or an active military person, "Hi! I'd like to listen to a story you might have." Follow up with, "Do you have a positive story about one of your experiences during your service?" This can set the tone of the listening opportunity by asking thoughtful questions. Another wonderful opening question for veterans and active military is, "What branch of military service have you served in or are you serving in?" That question will open the doors to many shared experiences. When we listen to another person who shares our similar views, work or passion, we listen more intently.

Another great method of listening is to imagine that the person is going to describe a scene from a movie. The story may have some very interesting facts and a different point of view. As you're listening, try to visualize what they are describing. It will help you to actually feel what the person is trying to communicate.

One essential point is that if the teller begins to go into the direction of negativity, it can be very difficult on the listener. It would then be sensible and supportive to say in the conversation, "I can tell this is a difficult part of your story for you, do you see a turnaround or positive aspect of your story?" You may be surprised by how effective this can be and how understanding the story teller is likely be with your compassionate suggestion. Perhaps they may even appreciate the new direction.

Listener, your job is to see the positive parts of the story and encourage the teller to enhance them. You will see how this dramatically benefits the teller.

Session Three

RELEASE

VLP Guide

The veteran tells their story, focusing on how they can release the negative and turn things around for the positive. The listener receives the story.

VLP Teller Guide

Session 3 places you on the right road and heading in the right direction with the Listening Post. VLP fully supports you. The driving purpose from now on is the empowerment of your stories. Steady-state story powers have arrived!

Release: Veteran's Story

Hello, Listening Post. This is Samantha 455. I am on this road with you. I'd like to tell you about a part of my National Guard service, when I was called up for service in 2005, during the Iraq conflict. My unit was responsible for a part of the security for the green zone in the Baghdad area of Iraq. *Green zone* is a military term that specifies an area that is relatively safe from insurgents and enemy forces. My unit saw its fair share of action throughout my thirteen month tour. At times, I thought it would never end. There were both good and tough times. It is the good times I choose to remember and the tough times I choose to let go. I guess you could say, that in the long run, I found some great buddies and learned some great lessons that I believe are helping me now on a daily basis. Thanks for listening. I needed to tell you this story.

Listener's Story and Response

Hi Samantha 455. I am David 301. You have a very healthy outlook on your time in the service. Thirteen months is a long time to be away from your home and your family. I admire how you have chosen to remember the good.

Also, the information you provided about the green zone is so interesting. You are a very good storyteller. Please continue with more stories.

VLP's Response

Samantha 455, very positive story. Continue with these aspects of releasing through sharing your story or another story, if needed. Stay with your guidelines and stay in the uplifting parts of your story.

Discussion Format

Effective releasing has huge power. Let the statements below express your positive direction. During the week, re-read your statements of positive influence.

VLP Release Affirmations

1. Yes, I have a turnaround story.
2. I'm creating a good story.
3. I am hoping I'll find more stories.
4. like working through my story.
5. Telling my story makes me realize how important I am in my own journey.

Personal and Universal Listening

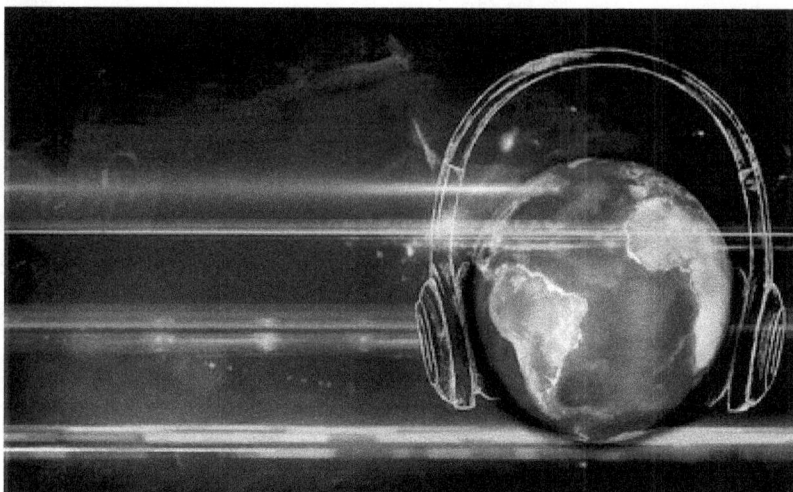

Personal listening happens in one-on-one and small group gatherings. It is the support that comes from family, friends and personal supporters through what VLP calls *opportune personal listening*. By looking for and having these occasions of opportune personal listening with veterans or active military will leave the teller and listener with positive experiences.

Universal listening is accomplished through large venues such as newspapers, magazines, live events, the Internet and social media. We make use of this power every day. One of VLP's universal-support statements states, "Be attentive and open to the avenues of communication that relate to veterans and military."

Our smartphones, laptops, tablets and all our other devices keep us connected. We spend a good part of our day using these devices. We can take the extraordinary power of these devices and turn it into a positive power for our veterans and military as universal listening opportunities arise.

When we read the newspaper, we gravitate toward the items that attract us such as the new fashions or the good deals on a restaurant for dinner. On occasion, there is a current news article regarding our veterans or the military. Just by reading these articles we become part of the universal-listening process, understanding more about our veterans and military. Much of the incoming information from newspapers and websites can be on the negative side. We can continue with the negative comments or we can be what VLP calls "a teller of positive turnaround." Positive turnaround is a statement that can buoy and uplift the intended audience in an affirmative way.

Even though there can be negative details in a newspaper or Internet article concerning veterans and military, there is always an approach that we can take with a vehicle of communication to turn around a negative story. We can turn around a negative story by finding the positive and turning it into uplifting comments that we can post. Despite these setbacks in negative articles or online posts, we say, "How about the amazing strength our veterans and military display, despite some downward viewpoint articles!" This is patriotism in action yielding positive outcomes.

When there are local events for veterans and active military in your town, attending them is universal listening. You do not have to know anyone. Just by standing there watching and participating, you are activating universal listening. You are displaying your patriotism. A veteran or military person will see you being supportive, and both of you will know, this is patriotism at its best!

Posting any type of positive statement about our veterans and our military on social media sites is one of the greatest forms of universal listening. Out of all the posts we will ever write, you will never regret a post with an uplifting, positive statement for the benefit of our veterans and active military.

Session Four

DIRECT

VLP Guide

The veteran tells their story with direction. The listener receives the story.

VLP Teller Guide

VLP is here with you in Session 4, and you are here with us. Good! Thank you! This is tangible progress and power. Let's begin this session with a new story, one with uplift. You have accomplished so much with your tours of duty and commitment to your country. Please proceed.

Direct: Active Military Member's Story

Hi, Listening Post! This is Susan 160. I have been listening to the VLP stories and would like to tell one of my own. As a single mother of two, you would think that it would be difficult to manage a family and rise to the goals that the army demands of its staff. Well, it is! I am still in the army after nine years and my goal is to make this my career. I am always juggling the responsibilities of my profession and my duties as a single mother. It is extremely difficult, yet with the tremendous support from the services of the army and my team members, I am able to have plenty of good things to say.

I live on post and receive army services on base, like housing and schooling for my children; this has helped me in fulfilling my duties to both my children and my country. I have attained the rank of Sergeant First Class. My neighbors, the army wives and my friends are an invaluable resource to me. They have helped me with my children and with time management.

I am glad that I can tell my story because it shows how much my support team has helped me. My story is "helping begets helping." I am so grateful for all the help that others have given me and I hope my story helps someone else. Thanks for listening, Susan 160.

Listener's Story and Response

Hello, Susan 160. Wow! What a story! This is Megan 220. You have put together connections between the events in your story that demonstrate to me the reason that you hold the rank of Sergeant First Class!

I love the phrase *juggling responsibilities*, it sounds like you know how to organize and manage yourself well. You talk mostly about how others in your life have helped you. You have a very generous spirit, full of gratitude and praise for others. Please continue with more stories. This one is great and very uplifting!

Discussion Format

Direct support from others is super uplifting. How do we convert our story into a vibrant support network in our lives? This week, try to visualize the stability and strength in your environment and find ways to express your direction.

VLP Direct Affirmations

1. I'm giving direction to my story.
2. I'm turning my good story into a positive and inspirational story.

3. I'm working on staying more focused.

4. I'm realizing what good sense it makes to be positive.

5. I'm becoming positive and accomplishing very good things that will help me with my with my steady-state story progress.

The Bus Ride

Have you ever experienced a long bus ride or taken a bus from uptown to downtown? When we exit the bus at the bus stop, we take a few seconds to reorient ourselves, to know where we are and what direction we want to proceed. Once we adjust to our surroundings, we develop a plan to proceed on the next step of our journey.

Imagine this bus ride! Thirty new recruits on a bus, and the last and only stop is United States Army Base, Basic Training Center, Fort Jackson Columbia, South Carolina. This bus stop is a real life-changer! As the recruits step off the bus, they are greeted by a U.S. Army Drill Sergeant. He is their new reorientation expert.

He makes it clear that at this bus stop, carefree tourism is not on the agenda.

The receiving drill sergeant, with an unmatched aura of leadership and command in his voice says, "Cruits!" This thunderous word vibrates through the recruits, shaking them to their core. Drill sergeants are the military's backbone. They are the trainers of transformation, ingraining the enduring strength one will need for military service.

The drill sergeant continues his "warm" welcoming speech, "Cruits, where do you think you are? You are now in my house, and in my house, nobody ever walks. You never walk in my house. You will always *run* in my house. Is that clear, "Cruits?"

The thirty new recruits, at this, unlike any other, bus stop, are stunned and stilled. The only two words that will work in this moment are, "Yes, Sergeant!"

One would think that this bus stop and the days that follow it are something to fear, but not so. The intensive training that follows this bus stop becomes a twelve week journey that transforms these bus riders, these recruits, into polished, performance-oriented American soldiers.

Making a decision to go in a positive direction, even at uncertain bus stops in life, opens innumerable doors and creates countless possibilities for positive outcomes in your life.

So, believe in the good possibilities when you are at uncertain stops and crossroads in life, and then be assured that good things will follow.

Session Five

HEALING

VLP Guide

The veteran tells a story of events they believe would produce healing for them. The listener is open and nonjudgmental, and receives their story.

VLP Teller Guide

Continue with your purpose in Session 5. This is going from good to great. Visualize moments, events and people that you want to have in your life as well as positive things that are not yet present in your life, but that you know will arrive. The Listening Post Network fully supports you

In this session, you are right in the middle of your wonderfully relevant story. Continue unfolding who you are and what you're made of. Make it stick. Say, "My story works right here and right now. My positive story continues arriving all the time."

Healing: Veteran's Story

Hi, VLP! Jack 261 here and Air Force all the way! I have been out of the U.S. Air Force for ten years now, but feel my story has some worth.

I called upon the strength that I developed in the Air Force to help me in this story.

While working in a job I loved, I found out that I was being phased out of a job that I had because of a pending sale of the company. At first, this was very troublesome for me. They gave me an ending date for my employment and told me to just continue working, until the other company's team came in and took over.

I could have been mad and quit and gone on my way, but I reached for that positive strength that I developed in my military service, to stay on course. I stayed on the job, doing my work diligently.

As the ending days approached, the transition team from the new company began their company's new operational agenda. I helped them put the fabric of their new network in place. When I left on my last day, I had completed my duties with integrity. Surprisingly, the next morning, I found a message on my phone from the new company's transition team. I called them back and well, this is where my story becomes very good!

The new team noticed my work ethic and integrity. They presented me with a significant opportunity to continue working for the new company. I took it! I even received a pay increase and I am now thrilled to be working with the new company's team. Air Force all the way! Thanks for listening, VLP. It was very good for me to share my story.

Listener's Story and Response

Jack 261, this is Darnel 242. Wow! What really stands out and what is so impressive about your story is that, when all those shaky and uncertain changes took place in your life, you did not bend to the negative news. You stayed and did what was required of you with unbelievable integrity. Wow! This is an amazing story! What a positive outcome! Great job!

Thanks for sharing your story!

Discussion Format

In our stories, we have the resilience and resources to handle any rough times that we may face. Stay steady and wait for certain events to line-up in your story so you can position yourself for the best outcomes and opportunities.

Embrace the statement or words below that best expresses your direction for healing and turnaround. This week do something good for yourself, and watch the healing aspects of your actions become actuality in your life.

VLP Healing Affirmations

1. I like giving support.
2. I like releasing my feelings, through telling my story.
3. I'm developing a healing story for myself.
4. I'm heading in the direction that I want to go.
5. My turnaround is working very well for me.

Section Two

The Neuroscience of Happiness

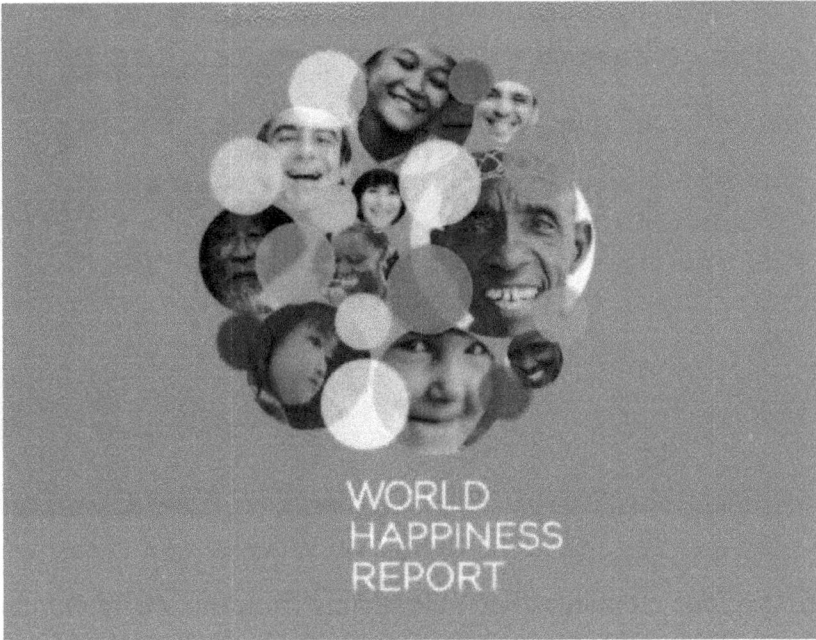

WORLD
HAPPINESS
REPORT

Sometimes, the word *happiness* can be taken lightly. We tend to think of happiness as something from the outside that comes into us. In many ways, we want to purchase happiness somewhere and bring it into us so we can be cheerful, blissful and ecstatic. However, there is another kind of happiness.

In the "World Happiness Report," produced by the Sustainable Development Solutions Network, it states that the word *happiness* is studied as a world-wide common lifestyle of well-being. VLP says, "Happiness continuously evolves and grows as one approaches a sustainably positive sense of well-being."

By *well-being*, we mean mental and physical health for our life's journey and maybe more. Well-being is the process of dynamic personhood. Dynamic personhood is one's steady-state story power, the ability to adapt and adjust for your beneficial well-being.

Elements of Well-Being

There are four elements that VLP affirms from the World Happiness Report that are guides for the development of sustained positive well-being.

The first of these elements is *generosity*. Generosity, for our purposes, means to be good to yourself while supporting conscious actions of positive influence that benefit your own goals of well-being.

The second element is being *pro-social. Pro*, in this context, means to advocate physical movement, exercise, sports and other physical hobbies. *Social* means the act of including other persons in those activities.

The third element is *recovery*. When a negative situation presents itself, there is a process within a person, within their natural well-being, that can absorb this circumstance. Taking a pause to relax and wait can give rise to a new re-set and turnaround. Recognizing different points of view can make ready your natural resources that are already built into you, to see a new story, a more positive story. This is *recovery*.

The fourth element is *release from effective stickiness*. Effective stickiness is when negative events that we experience, want to stick around and hold us captive to their influence. Using the tools of positive story rebalancing allows strong release effects to take hold, leaving effective stickiness ineffective, unstuck and with no power. (Sustainable Development Solutions Network)

Steady-State Story Process

An individual can potentially have high levels of well-being, yet not be happy every moment of the day. For example, a person might respond with feelings of frustration, sadness and other negative emotions while dealing with unsettling health issues, dysfunctional relationships and other outside disturbing events hindering their lives.

Therefore, developing a non-judgmental, matter-of-fact disposition gives them a powerful re-set point for their turnaround direction. With positive well-being at your core, you will find that these negative states become short-lived experiences. These emotional states will become opportunities and crossroads for that turnaround, uplift, and positive story. This can be maintained though the VLP steady-state story power process.

Session of Insight

In the foreword of this course book the meditation instructor said, "The person that goes into meditation, is not the same person that comes out of meditation."

By adding sessions of insight to the steady-state VLP teller and listener course, we increase our ability to have a turnaround with an uplifting and continuously positive story. The steady-state teller and listener course encourages you to develop your three-deep power resource. The three-deep power resources are *present power*, *re-set power* and *belief power*. This three-deep insight practice increases your ability to overcome negative stories and help reset the outcomes to create significantly positive stories.

An insight session is a cousin of meditation. The difference between a session of insight and a meditation session is the intended goal.

We all have natural meditation built into us. For instance, when we finish some long task or come to the end of a long day we like to just sit and relax. This is a form of meditation. Similarly, when we daydream about things we'd like to attain, this is also a form of meditation. When we do some real focusing and concentrating on a task in the present moment, this is also a kind of meditative state.

One of the solid takeaways when using insight sessions is that this method can be applied to other goals or aspects of one's life. If you practice some form of meditation, a session of insight will fit easily into your practice. These techniques draw upon valuable instinctual assets that we all have.

In this session of insight, we're using the VLP anchor words that have been supplied in the VLP course. These one-word guidelines and easy descriptions, when practiced regularly, blend quickly into each other. A session can be done at any time of the day or night. The important thing to remember is that, if you practice, it will serve you extremely well in your daily life.

Insight Session

Willpower

Setting aside a time and place to complete a session.

Intention

This is what we would like to happen, as an outcome, beyond the actual session. The intention of this session is the continuation of the positive outcomes that are already instituted within the VLP course structure.

Begin Session

Inhale and exhale deeply just one breath, then breathe naturally. You can do this with your eyes open or closed. Either way will work well.

In-Session

Begin by saying, within yourself, the word, **turnaround**, a few times. When ready, follow with the word, **uplift**. Then say to yourself the word, **positivity**. Say these words easily and slowly. Let the words flow, in and out, as a quiet stillness and clearness become part of the initial session's process.

Duration

A 10-minute session will work very well. You may use longer or shorter sessions as a personal preference.

Completion

Complete each session with a feeling of accomplishment. These sessions become cumulative with real effects materializing and producing more innovative ways of thinking. This fosters confident and constructive stories which will produce even more positive outcomes. When something transpires in your life that you want to change for your betterment, pause, and then say, turnaround, uplift and positivity. Watch as more positive outcomes and changes for the better begin to take root in your life.

Section Three

Basic Training

In one way or another, we all go through some type of basic training in our lives. It's a time and place where substantial changes occur, sending you on a different path.

Basic training in the US military is one of those challenging reset paths for those who dare to be great and plan to have a positive impact on their country.

An hour in military basic training might go something like this. At 4:45 a.m. the sounds of sleeping and snoring fill the barracks, which are amplified by those thirty guys just dropped off at the bus stop. The drill sergeant enters the barracks with the morning greeting: "Rise and shine! Rise and shine, gentlemen! Everybody up, up, up!" This is your champion drill sergeant in action. "Fall-in time is ten minutes!" (Fall-in means to be outside the barracks and dressed in uniform for the daily run). You may, for a moment, think this is a dream and in a few minutes you will wake up to your mother cooking you pancakes.

No such luck. "Run!" And run you will. Oh, and no fancy running shoes here. Combat boots all the way. Whatever is asked and ordered for you to do, the drill sergeant will do it first and all the while looking like he just came out of a tanning booth to show you just how easy things are in basic training.

The run will last close to an hour uphill, downhill, over roads and fields with no stopping. Until the drill sergeant decides to slow the run down into a marching cadence. The rhythm of this cadence goes something like this:

Left, left, left, right, left. Left, left, left, right, left.

Wanna go home on your left, You're right!
Wanna go home on your left, You're right!
Sound off, one, two, Sound off, three, four!
Bring it on down, one, two, three, four. One, two! Three, four!

Going through any type of basic training in life is tough; however this toughness will always chisel out new and rewarding changes.

The good thing about the run, in military basic training, is that you will wind up at the mess hall (cafeteria.) This turns out to be a very good thing, "FOOD!"

Non-Commissioned Officers Training

You might think that basic training would be the toughest training you could go through in the military. Well, think again! Like going from college to graduate school, the next course of action in military training requires plenty of effort for its completion. The drill sergeants who train our military in Non Commissioned Officers (NCO) training, and all other advanced training in the military seem to have come out of a time zone of absolute control and expertise. They know everything, do everything and always looked like they could manage and take charge of any situation that occurred in their life. These drill sergeants are similar to a good coach who inspires and gives you the direction that can propel you towards your life's greatest successes. The big advantage you have in moving to the next school or the next part of military training is that there is some depth of understanding and experience that you take with you from the prior training.

This is great because the candidates that show up for NCO School in the military are no slouches. When the drill sergeant says the run is at

4:30, the candidates are ready to run strong, solid and endurance style runs. When candidates perform maneuvers like rappelling down the training walls, they do it with courage that continues to grow and take hold, further developing their confidence.

When these soldiers stay up all night performing difficult night maneuvers, knowing the next day they will be doing more of the same, these candidates will say, "I got this, what's next?"

One of the duties of NCO training is being in charge for a day as a First Sergeant. This is an exacting task. When picked for this duty you are required to attend an established NCO meeting with the Lieutenants and Captain for the briefing on the protocol for the next day's training.

When the next morning comes, you are in the spotlight, calling the full company unit to order in a football-sized field. It goes something like this:

"COMPANY, A-ten-shun!"

Then the next command you will bark is :

"REPORT."

The platoon sergeants, one for each of the four platoons, snap a perfect salute. Each sergeant then reports:

"First platoon all present and accounted for."

"Second platoon all present and accounted for."

"Third platoon all present and accounted for."

"Fourth platoon all present and accounted for."

You, as the First Sergeant, with your best about-face, then turn, pause and salute the Company Commander (the Captain) saying:

"Sir, NCO Training Company, all present and accounted for, Sir!"

The Company Commander salutes and says:

"Carry on Sergeant."

Hmm, and that is just the beginning of the day!

Session Six

HEALTH

VLP Guide

The veteran tells a personal health story they believe would be healthy and healing for them to share. The listener receives the story.

VLP Teller Guide

Welcome to Session 6. The best is yet to come!

Embrace your capacity for endurance. See it as a pillar of strength that you can call up and rely upon when needed. Know that you have the resources in place to handle your present purpose, supporting healthy life outcomes. You have made it through some challenging times. Pat yourself on the back, hero! Now, let's hear a portion of that experience in your next story.

Health: Veteran's Story

Hello, VLP, this is Joe 277, reporting. Once a Marine, always a Marine. Many professions come with their difficulties. If you ask someone, "Would you do this job or that job?" Some people will say, "I'm not cut out for it." "It will take too much schooling." "It's just not one of my choices."

For me, however, a few actual challenging professions would be a heart surgeon, a jet fighter pilot, a monk, or even a rice-paddy farmer. These professions take time and endurance, not dissimilar to going through Marine training.

For me, boot camp and advanced training in the Marines fits within the category of challenging professions. If you ask most people, "Could you be a Marine?" The answer would be, "I wish, but I just couldn't endure the training." I believe part of staying healthy means constantly pushing toward your dreams, no matter what. My dream was to become a Marine, and I worked hard to become one. It took a lot of time, effort and endurance, but I got there, one step at a time.

It was very good for me to express this story.

Thanks so much for listening, VLP.

Listener's Story and Response

Hello, Joe 277. This is Dave 179. Semper Fi! Marine, you are the best of the best!

Yes, I am a Marine Veteran also. I look back and say, "How did I make it through Marine Basic Training on Parris Island in South Carolina?" We know the answer: grit, mental fortitude and courage.

I am a little heady and emotional with this story. I just wanted to thank you for your story. Thanks, Marine Dave 179.

Discussion Format

This story speaks for itself. During this week, describe your current health.

VLP Health Affirmations

1. I am skilled in staying healthy.
2. I'm always looking for healthy ways of living.
3. I know there are rewards for staying healthy.
4. Health is good listening, to good stories.
5. Health is what I do and what I believe in.

Sergeant Rock

The name, Sergeant Rock, readily exhibits the heroism of the sergeants of the United States Armed Forces. The name, Sergeant Rock, signifies courage and bravery.

In the 1950's, the American Comic Book Company seized this iconic display of bravery from the sergeants of recent wars and produced a comic book introducing the "Sergeant Rock" character and stories. This was a complete success for the American Comic Book Company.

Sergeant Rock's platoon-style military operations expertise provided the basis for handling any task in a story's mission. Sergeant Rock's consistent use of logic provided an approved baseline for daily conduct and demonstrated the practical application of his problem-solving skills. The common-sense mantra was consistently reinforced throughout the "Sergeant Rock" comic book series.

There is a part of the Sergeant Rock stories that is universal and is a part of all of our stories. Many of the stories about our lives, the lives of veterans and active military are stories that have distress, fear, shock and loss woven into them. Many stories include heroism, luck, magic and miracles. In most heroic movies, we see the hero get pummeled, crushed and flattened. It seems, for the moment, that there is nothing left of our hero. You might say, "That's the end of that hero." However, there is always an uplifting moment in these stories, a turnaround, a small action of sacrifice, perseverance and endurance, when the hero of the story, the Sergeant Rock who resides in all of us, turns this seemingly lost and forgone story into a new and better present story.

No, it's not easy, but what hero's story is? Through small acts of telling and listening to a new story, a tough, hopeless mission can turn into a positive, successful mission.

Session Seven

STABILITY

VLP Guide

The veteran tells their story of how they will support that which keeps their story healing and healthy. The listener will receive the story.

VLP Teller Guide

You are now in Session 7. This is where we know that more positive outcomes are possible. Tell your story about your present time. Stay in the present. It's where your story will become you.

Stability: Veteran's Story

Hi, VLP! Just call me, POP 450. I am a World War II Veteran. I wonder if soon they will be calling World War II "ancient history." That's okay with me. My training long ago has served me well. In World War II, the U.S. Navy needed what they called construction battalions or Seabees. When I entered the Navy, I knew nothing at all about construction.

I developed my skills through the excellent training I received, on-the-job experience and my involvement with tough naval operations. Fast-forwarding to the present, I am now living on a well-deserved pension that started with construction from my naval training. I've been living well and really having fun telling my story.

Good job, VLP!

Listener's Story and Response

POP 450, this is Dave 901. I'm in the construction industry and reading your story gives me goose bumps. I get so much strength and purpose from your story. You represent the heart of construction workers. We are the part of America that works very hard with much physical labor and effort.

Construction has its challenging times, but when you go to work and do your part, you always feel this deep sense of self-worth and satisfaction. You walked the solid walk, POP 450. Thanks so much for your story.

Discussion Format

What does it take to stay on course? Which affirmations express stability? Rely on a friend this week. Let friends rely on you.

VLP Stable Affirmations

1. Small moves build long, steady roads.
2. Starting right now is being steady.
3. I like my direction toward the positive.
4. I'm creating a new story, when needed.
5. If I uplift others, it will uplift me.

The Saint Christopher Effect

There are many similarities between our veterans and military and the characteristics of Saint Christopher. There are many different stories and legends about the man named Saint Christopher. What has been written about Saint Christopher, in some chronicles, is how he performed many very extraordinarily positive services for people during his lifetime.

He was known for his unwavering loyalty, dedication, and physical strength. Saint Christopher lived during a time in history when actions like crossing a river were a perilous activity. Unsavory people routinely took advantage of travelers. Most people in Saint Christopher's time were concerned only with protecting themselves. After all, going further out of one's way to help someone else could be very dangerous.

After repeatedly going through troubling situations during his own life, Saint Christopher saw another story for himself, one of helping others, and this became his life's purpose. He built his story around a course of service to others. He rose to the challenge to produce positive outcomes for himself and others. It is these legendary stories that resulted in his sainthood.

The most notable of Saint Christopher's abilities and services were helping others to cross rivers. During that time of history, bridges were almost non-existent. Crossing a river, unaware of the hazardous currents and its unexpected depths, could present a life-threatening struggle to survive.

Saint Christopher's call of service, to help those in need of river crossings, was his gift. Some stories say he possessed miraculous abilities which he employed when helping others cross dangerous rivers. Saint Christopher stood strong in his belief to serve others.

We can see the undeniable comparisons of Saint Christopher and our veterans and military. Take for instance the Oath of Service a military woman or man takes when entering the military. Military personnel promise to serve and defend their country when they take the Oath of Service.

The Oath could be summed up like this: regardless of political views, race, religion or any other diverse sides that we Americans may take, the military person will defend the country and you from any harm. This service of our veterans and present military, their sacrifice, strength and protection are the river crossings of strength and perseverance that back up the freedom of the United States of America and the free world.

Because of this impartiality and dedication of service that we can readily see in our veterans and military men and women, we can see that the Saint Christopher effect is alive and well and is continuously displayed with a strong resolve that will never fail.

Today we view Saint Christopher as the protector of travelers. We now proudly proclaim that our veterans and military are our, "Saint Christophers of freedom."

Section Four

Session Eight

SUPPORT

VLP Guide

When resistance comes, develop a turnaround.

VLP Teller Guide

Here we begin Session 8. The Listening Post is always on call to support you in your continued steady-state story purpose.

Support: Veteran's Story

How's it going VLP? I'm Barry 710. At the beginning of my basic training, I was one of those grunts, a little slower at picking up the training maneuvers that were required to pass basic training. The physical training was the toughest. I just couldn't pass that low-crawl physical test within the required time. As we moved into the weeks of training, there was this super athletic guy who became my friend in the same platoon. I called him Big G. He took me under his wing.

He examined my low-crawl and said these words, that helped me immensely, "The low-crawl has a lot to do with just a good technique." With Big G's coaching and practicing how to use my forearm as the pushing strength for the low-crawl, I realized that I could move at a much faster pace.

I passed all the physical tests in basic training with Big G's help.

I salute you, Big G, wherever you are! It is because of you that I am here telling this story.

Thanks, VLP. I really enjoyed sharing this experience.

Listener's Story and Response

Hello, Barry 710. This is Sally 455. Wow, to you! You have a great story about people rising and helping one another during their military service days.

The amazing thing about your story is how opposite types of people can join forces to make things better for all. Just a super story!

Hey, is Big G out there? This is Sally 455. I'm available. LOL

VLP's Response

Continue with those positive aspects of your story or, if needed, another story. Stay within your guidelines. Stay with what is working.

Discussion Format

Veterans, military and civilians, we are all one in our support. Patriotism = Support = The Power to be Free.

This week, take an opportunity that comes your way to help support someone else. This week, ask for support when you need it. It will come.

VLP Support Affirmations

1. Yes, I have a support story.
2. I'm creating a good story.
3. I'll use more stories when needed.

4. I like working through my story.

5. Telling my story makes me realize just how important I am in my own journey.

Rock Star vs. Military

Have you ever met a rock star, movie star or athletic star? If not, how do you imagine it might make you feel? Perhaps, something like this: You are walking down your hometown's main street, very relaxed, when you notice a person a short distance away who looks very familiar. You see and recognize this person coming towards you as a very famous movie star. Your heart starts to beat faster, your legs go wobbly, you get all flushed and you giggle.

The movie star looks at you and says, with a big smile, "Hi!" Then starts up a conversation, asking you for some advice on where there's a pleasant restaurant to eat at in town. You pass on your best advice, with all your charm. The movie star thanks you, telling you that you have been very helpful and asks you to keep in touch through a phone number exchange.

Wow! As soon as you take the next few steps from this encounter you are texting and calling your family, friends and even people you don't know to tell them all about how you are now friends with a movie star. You know what? It is right to share a very positive experience and story that is uplifting for others to hear.

A new story opportunity arises. You are in an airport, maybe a store, a restaurant or any public place. As you glance up, there is a United States military person or veteran, in uniform, walking into your view. As this person comes closer, displaying with their uniform their commitment to public service and freedom, does your heart beat a little faster? Will your eyes open a little wider? This military person, who we do not even know, is defending not only our country, but is defending us personally every day.

The uniform worn by this person is a representation of all that we consider to be sacred and secure. Now, when the opportunity arises and you see or pass by a military serviceperson in their wonderful uniform, you can view them just like you would an athletic star, rock star or movie star.

You can smile wide and strong. We are seeing our security and freedom in action. The rock star, athletic star, movie star, veterans and military are all stars and heroes in their own way.

Session Nine
CONFIDENCE

VLP Guide

The veteran tells a story about the firmness and stability that is present in their life. The listener receives the story.

VLP Teller Guide

We now begin Session 9. Let's talk about a "Seasoned person" and an "experienced person." These are phrases which express how capable someone is and the resources that are a part of a person's continuous story.

At this juncture, your attributes are sustainable. Rise and show, through your story, that there is firmness and stability in your steady-state story power.

Confidence: Active Military Member's Story

Hello, VLP. This is Logan 224. I really need and enjoy listening to the VLP stories. They are very therapeutic for me. I have a story for you. As I put on my uniform every day, there is an uplift of confidence that surges through me and leads me into what I call, "My Performance Story."

My performance story is all my training and the uplifting leadership I receive being in the military.

Deep, down, inside of me, I am aware that my story is part of something very important for the freedom of my country and for the world.

This awareness gives me what you at VLP call, "steady-state purpose," to do my part to serve, to do that part that no one else can do, but me. I am so thrilled to tell my story. So much thanks, Logan 224.

Listener's Story and Response

Hi, Logan 224. This is Joanne 620. My son serves in the Coast Guard. Your story is dazzling. I cannot thank you enough for the service that you provide for our country. Yours is such a delightful story. Oh, and keep putting that uniform on every day. You are a defender of freedom!

With love,
Joanne 620

VLP's Response

Let's just savor the beauty of this story.

Discussion Format

Firmness and confidence should rule your being. What part of your life is confident and firm? Which statement below helps you stay going in a positive direction? The statements below are your arsenal of confidence, use them. They will support and defend you.

VLP Confident Affirmations

1. I'm certain about my patriotism.
2. I'm looking to build my decisiveness.

3. "Steady-state story purpose" is what I want.
4. My goal is to be consistently balanced.
5. I am confident, firm and reliable.

Listening to Iraq and Afghanistan Veterans

The mission statement of the United States Navy is, "A force for good." These few words, sum up beautifully, a picture of thousands of ships, planes, men, women and equipment traversing the earth's oceans. All of these are displaying the strength and military might of the United States of America for the protection of our country and the free world. We want to show all of our military protective services stationed in Iraq, Afghanistan and all around the world, that we are firmly behind them and fully support their bravery, service and sacrifice.

Now, more than ever, we must do things like connect, encourage, cheer and support our veterans and military. It is important that we honor those who have served with our own actions of patriotism, in everyday real-time displays that uplift and support all the different mission statements of our military.

Vietnam Veterans developed their own mission statement when they came home, during the Vietnam era. When meeting another Vietnam Veteran at home, the saying to each other was, "Welcome home, brother." This statement was born out of the fact, that at the time, receiving a welcome home was somewhat unpopular for Vietnam Veterans.

Presently, the statement, "Thank you for your service," has come to represent all veterans and military services. It rings especially true for the Iraq and Afghanistan Veterans, as well as all military currently serving.

"Thank you for your service," was born out of the goodness of our civilians wanting to show, in a very positive way, their support for our returning veterans and military.

While this statement shows its worth in many ways, adding more ways of showing support and recognition for our present military service people is very important. More statements and sayings of support will constantly revitalize the flame of recognition.

We want to display, say and demonstrate, as many times as we can, that we connect with, recognize and support our active military and veterans. Let's be very bold with our statements. Let's say, "Veterans and military, you are the lights of freedom."

VLP says that the Iraq and Afghanistan Veterans and all who are currently serving around the world are part of a very unselfish generation of servicemen and servicewomen, who have served, and are serving for all of the world's freedom.

Session Ten

COMPLETION

VLP Guide

The veteran describes the progress of their steady-state story. Unleash the power you have for healing, healthy and happy stories that have developed through this course. The listener receives the story.

VLP Teller Guide

Welcome to Session 10. Session 10 is not the end of the VLP listening course because there is no end to recognizing the turnaround, uplift and positivity in the stories that you have boldly created for your own benefit.

We at the Listening Post are in awe of your stories and participation.

Completion: Veteran's Story

VLP! Hello, this is David 601. This course is very real for me. I started as one person and I am finishing as another person. You made me realize, through this course, the worth and the strength of the authentic me.

When being discharged, I landed in Oakland, California and went through the discharge process there. On the flight home, I must have dreamed of a hundred different wonderful scenarios that would occur when I got home.

What made me the happiest on that flight home was that I was going to see all the people and all those places that I took for granted before. Now, I couldn't wait to see them and visit them all again.

When I first got home, I had a story to tell, but did not want to impose it on my family and the people I knew. The ups and downs were tough. The thing I have realized, with the help of this course, is that I really can change my story, transforming me from that **why-me person** into a positive **go-to person.** You know, when people take the time to listen to us vets and military, there is such a wonderful feeling of recognition and appreciation.

Really, it's nothing short of miraculous. I would like to say, much thanks to all of you who take the time to be listeners. I enjoyed every session and I will stay connected to the VLP cause forever.

VLP, Rocks!

VLP's Story and Response

David 601. This is VLP. You mirror the positive outcomes that we all want for our veterans, military and ourselves. All participants and readers of this course can focus, each day, on creating a more healing, healthy and happy story. Isn't the body always working on healing? Isn't it natural to try to keep ourselves healthy? Isn't happiness our inner steady-state story?

Discussion Format

Let's pour out some large doses of forgiveness for others and ourselves. Let's also pour out some gratitude for those in our support networks because they are always giving and trying. Please always include large doses of humor and laughter. Thanks for posting your stories. Let us continue forevermore!

VLP Evermore Affirmations

1. Turnaround-uplift, expressions of success forevermore.
2. Significant improvement forevermore.
3. Positive outcomes forevermore.
4. Continuous support forevermore.
5. Positive well-being forevermore.

Taking Hold of Your Command

In the submarine movie, U-571, there is a quick change of command during wartime circumstances. The First Officer becomes the Captain. His start, as Captain, is somewhat shaky.

He delivers commands that are indecisive. The Chief of the boat, as they are called in the Navy, senses this and asks the Captain for permission to speak freely which the Captain grants. The Chief of the boat is straightforward and says, "Captain, if you are going to lead this command then lead with precision and decisiveness, no in-between." The Captain, going forward, leads brilliantly with precision, decisiveness and with a steady-state power of command.

We at the Veterans Listening Post would like to thank you for reading this course book. It would be remiss of VLP not to mention that in our world today, more than ever, it is important that we take care of our own and celebrate all who have made a difference in their communities and their country.

By reading this course book you are now a valued VLP listener. You will see the positive change that also occurs in you, just by listening. You are now part of the pass-it- forward mission to connect and recognize for our veterans, military and ourselves.

Bibliography

Helliwell, J., Layard, R., & Sachs, J. 2017,
World Happiness Report 2017
New York: Sustainable Development Solutions Network.
http://worldhappiness.report

Kanigher, Robert, and Kubert, Joe. "Our Army at War"
Cartoon. American
Comic Books. DC Comics. June 1959, #83

Sustainable Development Solutions Network. (2017)
http://unsdsn.org

U-571. Dir. Jonathan Mostow. Perf. Matthew McConaughey, Bill Paxton,

Harvey Keitel, Jon Bon Jovi, Jake Weber Universal Pictures 2000

The Listening Post National Guide

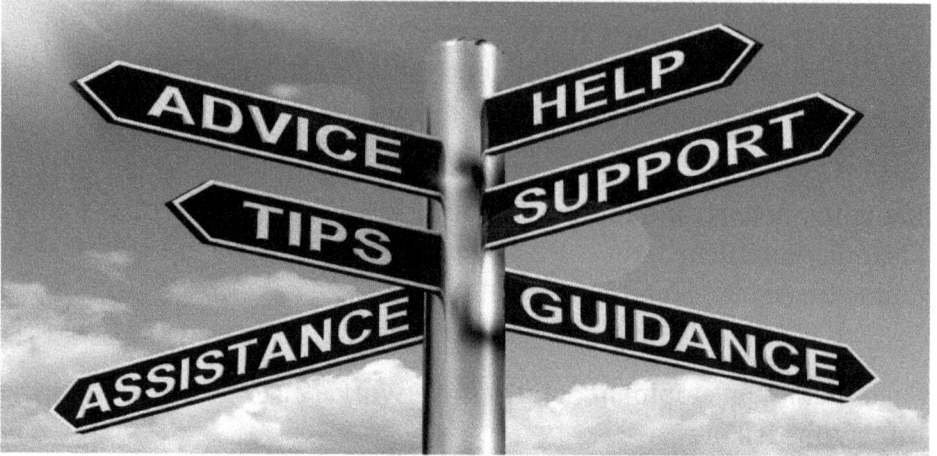

VLP's Programs of Influence

- On-the-ground action teams of listeners
- Positive-listening phone communication through answering-service platforms
- Website real-time interaction for tellers and listeners
- Teaching the ten-step transformation teller and listener program
- Veteran-recovery peer-specialist programs

Each program works independently of the others. Each platform serves a different type of need for veterans, military and civilians. Some veterans do not have readily available access to the Internet, but have a phone. Some veterans have no phone, but through word of mouth and local advertisement, they can find a safe place to meet with on-the-ground VLP service listeners. These three services can be used all together or one at a time.

The Listening Post communicates in three ways: group listening posts in local areas set up by VLP service representatives, phone conversations with representative listeners and online writings or voice communication through the story-coordination network. A three-minute action time for the voice process seems to work well for both tellers and listeners. While for writings, we look for installments of two pages or less.

On-the-Ground Action

In keeping with a military style of deployment, action teams of listeners at selected sites in local neighborhoods or at national venues can be mobilized very quickly to form a ready reaction force for on-the-ground action listeners. The Listening Post's sustainable goal is a VLP listening post in every local neighborhood, providing easy listening environments plus having a variety of information available that may be needed to direct veterans to the services they may need.

Team leaders, team listeners and individual listeners will be lightly trained because most of the required skills are patience and compassion as well as a desire to be part of a patriotic journey for the good for our veterans and military. Teams are made up of at least two people or as many as will further the action plan in place for the appointed day.

Hot spots are organized through small marketing campaigns, directed to pre-planned locations by a qualified listening-post team. Having small marketing campaigns will inform local veterans and active military that a listening post will be available in their area at certain locations on certain dates and times. It should be a fun and happy time, a celebration. No need to wait for Veteran's Day or Memorial Day. The time for action is now!

After the completion of the 10-session course, there are monthly meetings of support where the teams bring their own uplifting stories of their present journey to the meeting. Individual mentoring, group mentoring and facilitator trainings should be in action at all times. VLP calls this the airborne method, always jumping in to help! It is the only and best program in the country for what VLP calls accentuating the positive for veterans, military and civilians.

VLP Course Continuation

Listening-Course Resource Guide
Steady-State Story Process

The words and phrases to follow are statements of belief. Read them often and watch the turnaround, uplift and positive stories in your life become your real-life's story.

Session 1	Sharing	Tell your chosen story
Session 2	Purpose	Direct your story
Session 3	Release	Clean slate
Session 4	Direct	Change your story for beneficial good
Session 5	Healing	Upgrade to a better story as needed
Session 6	Health	Pro-social activites
Session 7	Stability	Stay on course with your story
Session 8	Support	Actions of influence
Session 9	Confidence	Assure expectations
Session 10	Completion	Steady-state journey

Session of Insight:

Will	Action of the mind that initiates the insight
Posture	Noble presentation, sitting with purpose
Intention	Beneficial purpose in mind
Concentration	Attention and focus
Imagination	Creates the journey
Breathing	Present moment
Session in Session	Words of alignment
Re-set to Belief	Support and centering
Duration	Time-in, time-out
Completion	Accomplishment and finishing point

HHH: Healing, Healthy, Happy Life

Healing Listening   Words of Encouragement Can Heal
Healthy Listening   Beneficial Environment
Happy Listening   Sustained Well-Being

The Four Elements:

Generosity   Good to Oneself
Pro-Social   Fun with Others
Recovery   Always Uplift
Release Power   Present Purpose

The Four Paradigms of Service:

Story Social   Shared Resources
Story Unity   Many Options
Internal Story   Building from Within
Sustainable Story   Inner Actions of Positive Influence

Core Words of Success:

Turnaround   Fresh Start, Brave New Beginning
Uplift   Steady Course
Recovery   Courageous
Positivity   Passionate, Enthusiastic, Gifted

Add all these words to your daily life and watch the changes multiply for your betterment.

Certificate of Support

Download your free VLP listener Certificate of Support at:
www.vlpost.com

This certificate can be personalized with your name, your business or organization.

A highly visible certificate is a wonderful way of displaying your support for veterans and military.

Looks great when printed on photo paper and framed.

Place the certificate on any social platform, as an expression of your support.

Coach Chris Uzzi

Chris Uzzi is the founder of Veterans Listening Post (VLP), a positive veterans' support organization and is a Service-Disabled Veteran-Owned, small business owner, supporting the Veterans & Military Listening Post, a 501(c)(3) non-profit.

"Coach", as Chris likes to be called, served in the United States Army as a Staff Sergeant during the Vietnam War, where he earned two Bronze Stars, a Combat Infantrymen's Badge, Vietnam Service medal, and the New York State Conspicuous Service Award.

He is a certified Veterans Recovery Peer Specialist, a certified Professional Life Coach and a Drug and Alcohol Treatment Specialist. Coach is currently the director of VLP's infrastructure and coaches through www.veteranslifecoaches.com, using the life-improvement service method.

He also directs, teaches and lectures on the VLP course book for the Pass-it-Forward Mission of VLP. Coach and VMLP provide counseling for the Jobless Warrior Program. One of Coach's passions is being involved as the Director of the Veterans' Activity Program that helps veterans through the pro-social activities as Veterans Director for Tropical Wheel Chair Sports and Pickleball for All, a 501(c)(3) non-profit, helping veterans through the game of pickleball.

E-mail Coach at coachchrisu@aol.com for further information or to request any help you may need.

VLP's Certifications and Services:

Certifications :

- US Federal Contractor Cage code 7FLF7 duns # 079646602
- Veterans Affairs Verification and Certification (SDVOSB)
- Veterans Enterprise Vendor and non-profit Ch51355
- Wainwright Institute of Professional Coaching
- Drug and Alcohol Treatment Stratford Career Institute
- Veterans Peer Recovery Program (CRPS100032)

Educational Services:

- VLP Guest Lecture Series for Personal and Universal Listening Techniques.
- Instructional seminars and certification for the Ten-Step Teacher Program for *Veterans—Military—Civilians: A Positive-Listening Course.*
- VLP provides programs for veterans' organizations, government agencies, private-help agencies, addiction centers, schools, college-forum classes, non-profits and personal motivational speakers. VLP also provides health and wellness programs such as yoga, insight meditation, emotional freedom techniques and other related programs.

Platforms of Services:

- Veterans & Military Listening Post
  www.vlpost.com
- Veterans Counseling for Jobless Warriors
  www.joblesswarrior.org
- Life Coach Center Point Method of Coaching
  www.veteranslifecoach.com

- Silver Lining Villages Veteran's Holistic Services www.silverliningvillages.com

- Pickleball for All (pro-social veterans' pickleball programs and services) www.pickleballforall.org

- Wheelchair tennis and pickleball programs www.tropicalwheelchairsports.org

SUPPORT

Invitation

VMLP invites you, your business, or organization to become a supporter and partner of the VMLP teller and listener programs for positive outcomes.

Expressions of support in any manner you think may help the VLMP mission are invited. Further interest and/or exchange of information as well as additional discussions are always welcome.

Now, more than ever, positive programs of support are vital for our veteran, military and civilian communities.

www.vlpost.com

Veterans & Military Listening Post
2430 Vanderbilt Beach Rd., Suite 108-135 Naples, FL. 34109
Fiscal Sponsorship Upon Request.
Organizations, Nonprofits and Personnel requests to:
veteranlistening@aol.com

www.ingramcontent.com/pod-product-compliance
Lightning Source LLC
Chambersburg PA
CBHW072045040426
42447CB00012BB/3030